The Cluster Of Thoughts

A Constellation Of Poems

Nanaki Bhatia

BookLeaf Publishing

India | USA | UK

Dedication

To little children, dreaming of writing books.

Preface

The tiny readers reading this inspired me to write a book so they can read poems anywhere and anytime. I also remember, when I was in 2nd grade, our teacher asked us to learn a poem written by a famous author and at that time I only knew one; Daffodils by William Wordsmith. Now I know many poems.

I hope everyone enjoys reading this!

Acknowledgements

To my mother, who stayed by my side the whole time,

To my teacher Ms Brar, who encouraged me,

And to Homer, who made the concept of poems.

1. LIFE ON MARS

I want to go to Mars, in a spaceship gazing at the stars.
The red planet has 2 moons, Phobos and Deimos, names
sounding like distant tunes.
You'll go flying because of gravity, that's the best
activity.
But sadly, you will feel lonely.
Unless aliens are real, then they will come to you asking
for a meal.
But if for the aliens, you don't have a meal of glory, then
that's another story.
We made it this far, on Mars.
Although it's time to go back home, so your family
doesn't feel alone.
And when you wake up in the morning, thinking it was
a dream.
You'll have a picture of yourself on Mars, gazing at the
stars.

2. THE LITTLE ALICORN

Once upon a time, there was an alicorn that gave birth to a little foal named Luna. The foal had a white body, a rainbow mane, a silver horn, golden hooves, and rainbow eyes. The little foal made lots of friends.

Then one day, when it was winter, men came into the jungle and all the animals hid, but the little foal didn't know where to hide. Suddenly, a man came and found the little foal and took her to their home. Once the men retreated, the animals came out. The foal's mother was worried, but it was too dangerous to look for the foal. The men kept the foal safe. The years passed, and the foal grew into a beautiful alicorn.

The men thought they had to spend too much time taking care of the alicorn, so the men let the alicorn go. Eventually, the alicorn found her way back to her mystical home. When she was back, her mother hugged her and the alicorn lived happily ever after with her family and her friends.

3. THE OLD MAN'S PAN

Once there was an old man's pan,
It looked like it was made of tin cans.
It was all crusty,
And a little musty.
The old man went to Hawaii and got tan without the
pan.

4. THE SCARED SCARECROW

Once upon a time, in a land full of fields and farms, there was one farm that had all the crops growing, everywhere, all the time. That farm had the highest amount of crops growing, but there was one problem, crows would come and wilt the crops or eat the berries! The farm owner built a scarecrow and named it Upca. The scarecrow was built with love and care, so it seemed almost alive! But, not ALMOST, he was alive! Every night, he wept about being unable to scare the crows, which was his job. Every night, he also wished he could have a brain!

He sang this poem every night:

"THE THINGS I COULD ACHIEVE WITH A BRAIN"

If I only had a fraction of a brain, oh the wonders that I could do are smarter than all of you!

Doo doo doo

Smarter than all of you.

With just a fraction of a brain!

Dun dee doo
If I only had a slight fraction of a brain, we would be jumping over rainbows and soaking the sun from our terrain.
If I only had a slight, fraction of a brain.

———————————————————————————

———————————————————————

One day, when the master's maiden was outside, she saw the scarecrow was not "scaring crows"! She called the master and he had to put the scarecrow in the closet room cupboard.

After a few years, the master sold the farm to a young man named Tom and his daughter, Zara. While exploring, Zara opened the cupboard and to her surprise, she found a scarecrow made of hay. After a few minutes of staring, Zara was about to leave when she heard someone say "WAIT! DON'T LEAVE ME" She thought she was dreaming and quickly pinched herself to check, but, it wasn't a dream! A scarecrow, talking! She ran fast and told her dad and he knew exactly what this was. He sat down with the scarecrow and began telling them a story. It was more like a myth but it was very heartwarming.

"Once upon a time" he began, there was a man who felt lonely and sad, sitting quietly in his cottage. So he built something out of hay, a scarf, sticks, a hat, some clothes, shoes, and some love. That was the first scarecrow ever to be built. The scarecrow's was named Rohn. Somehow it started moving, walking, and talking. But Rohn was sad because he couldn't scare the crows. Upca immediately said to Tom and Zara "That's how I feel".

Tom continued the story after smiling at Upca. Rohn was special, but people were mean to him as he couldn't scare anyone. However, Rohn's creator, Adam, made Rohn feel better and loved. Rohn knew he meant a lot to his creator Adam.

The moral of the story is "Pay attention to those who love thy, and ignore those who don't." said Tom. Upca told Zara about being sad for not having a brain and Zara told Upca how it felt with a brain and assured him not to feel sad if he doesn't have one as he only needs a heart to love. Tom, Upca, and Zara always stayed together.

5. THE PEACEFUL FOREST

I went outside for a walk and saw a forest;
I saw a crescent moon, the stars twinkling and my
shadow beneath my eyes.
The owls hooting quietly, the dandelions nearby,
Watching the waves walk along, making rush in the
peaceful night.
I went over to the beaming fireflies, making light in the
dark moonlit night.
A majestic deer pranced further to the lake drinking the
water, making the lake more stunning.
The scent of pine filled the air, making me feel more
debonair.
The stars twinkled brighter, as the night sky's blue got
deeper.
The life around me was so out of the box, looking
unexplainably attractive,
Each feature of the forest was unraveling in my mind.
In this woodland heaven, everyone has a place.
Nature's beauty makes me feel like I am in a dreaming

gaze.
This walk in nature made my soul walk back home,
"And if you look the right way, you see the whole world
is a garden,"
"If you truly love nature, you can see the beauty in
everything."
This walk to the forest made me realize:
Nature's beauty will beat everything in beauty, love, and
more you can find in the world,
And in nature, you won't see pain, you won't see vain,
and you won't see anything that you feel bad to lose.

6. THE CAKE WITH A WEIRD TASTE

I can't eat the cake with the weird taste.
But mom said not to waste.
So I threw it out,
Hopefully mom won't pout.
About me throwing out the cake with a weird taste.

7. MY CHESS MATCH

Chess is a complex game, you won't know if you don't
use your brain.
Black and white squares, when playing don't listen to
anyone's dares.
Save your king, and when you hear a ding.
It means you're out of time, but that's not a crime.
Bishop to B4, someone is knocking on the door.
Oh great, it's checkmate!

8. PIANO IN PARIS

Piano in Paris, don't feel embarrassed.
If you're the one playing, just keep on praying.
That you don't mess up, on seeing a cute little pup.
You have notes like C and B, don't fret if you see a bee.
And going on to the note B-baguette!
Don't get distracted by French food, I'm not trying to be crude.
So go on with playing songs like Clair De Lune, with a calming tune.
Für Elise, a beautiful piece.
And when you're finished, remember there is always more to play, later in the day.

9. CHILDHOOD DAYS

Don't you love those childhood days?
Fluttering around, acting in plays.
The problems were solved in the blink of an eye,
And a job well done is when you try.
All those chocolate drops,
And good days with pops.
Playing in the rain,
Without any vain.
Thinking of taxes,
But never having to pay!
Don't you just love those childhood days?

10. SCHOOL LIFE

Exams and homework,
It's a lot of hard work.
X=y=z=v + 3-9=13
But teacher how do we do it?
I don't get this bit.
When will it be lunchtime?
I'm just here for the bell's chime.
Children may whisper,
But no more whimpers.
You go home and gossip and have the time of your life.
Until you realize there is homework and an exam the
next day,
And you cannot play.

11. DESERT OR DESSERT?

Desert or dessert?
It's a question where you need to be alert.
Deserts are the hot place,
And dessert is the thing on your plate.
Which do you choose?
If you're a camel or a cactus,
I suggest choosing the desert.
If you're a kid like me,
Then you know the answer already.
So tell me, desert or dessert?

12. CHICKENS MATTER

C hickens matter, for our tummies and for Earth,
H old your horses, all the vegetarians,
I want to be veg, but I can't resist the smell of fresh fish,
C ooked and ready, perfect for pizza,
K ings eat chicken for breakfast, lunch and dinner,
E veryone come to the dinner table,
N ow we all have to become veg because that is what
mom said.

13. CROOKED TEETH

Crooked teeth, crooked teeth, when will you grow out?
If you don't, I will start to pout.
It looks a little weird, and I'll never be feared,
By the bullies and liars roaming about.
I guess it looks cute,
Like a bunny.
I hope no one says I look funny.

14. HOME

Home sweet home,
Filled with garden gnomes.
Over there I hold a special place,
And there is always a familiar face.
I feel debonair over there,
Knowing everyone will care.
We always learn good manners,
Sometimes with banners.
Just always remember,
Home is here forever.

15. TANGLED STARS

Tangled stars in the sky,
Struggling to untangle as people go by.
They shine so bright,
In the moonlight.
White or silver on dark blue,
People think they are just new.
They try so hard to untangle themselves,
People print their pictures and put them on shelves.
They are real that is true,
I know you all love them too.

16. BEAUTIFUL DAY

It is a beautiful day, am I right?
With a perfect amount of sunlight.
The ballerinas are dancing gracefully,
The poetess is writing beautifully.
The wind is whistling through the trees,
Everyone feels a peaceful breeze.
The neighbours are wishing everyone a good morning,
But the weather is transforming.
With thunder and rain,
But it didn't even last long enough for a penny gain.

17. STUDYING IN SCHOOL

Studying in school,
It helps you not to become a fool.
You do your homework,
So that one day you can become an office clerk,
Buy new pencils,
And new stencils.
You find a way to deal with your bully,
But never fully.
Just focus on your studies,
And talk to your buddies.

18. MY FRIENDS

My friends, My friends,
Who I play with on my mood that depends.
They comfort me all day,
And together we all play.
I meet them in school,
And together we play duels.
I love playing with my friends all day long,
And I love helping each other right our wrongs.

19. RAINY DAYS AND RAINBOWS

Rainy days and rainbows,
A time when I let go of my sorrows.
I play in the rain,
And see a construction crane.
We go in for a bite,
And lose our electric light.
It's all dark,
And we can only feel the wet bark.
Just a wolf howl,
To make a horror story that ends in a growl.
The rain stops,
There are just a few water drops.
The light is back on,
And thunder is gone.
A rainbow is in the sky,
Its so pretty that you want to cry.

20. TEA KETTLE

Tea kettle, tea kettle whistling away,
Into a cup, you get poured and the cup is on a tray.
Tea kettle, tea kettle whistling away,
I'll sip you one day.
Tea kettle, tea kettle whistling away,
Newborn British children will be drinking you for the
2nd time today.
Tea kettle, tea kettle whistling away,
Its nice to eat you with biscuits on a rainy day.
Tea kettle, tea kettle whistling away.

21. POEM PENDING

My poem is pending,
Because I need to give it some mending.
Time is running out,
But I wont pout.
I will write it fast,
With a vocabulary so vast.
What do I do,
It is almost two.
I knew what to write it on,
But my mind is blanking and my memory is gone.
Finally its done,
Now I can run.
To play with my friends in the sun.

www.ingramcontent.com/pod-product-compliance
Lightning Source LLC
LaVergne TN
LVHW010847200726

843508LV00012B/2786

9 789363 305816